Lift Up Your Hearts

Songs for Creative Worship

Linda White, editor

Pew Edition

Geneva Press
Louisville, Kentucky

Cover design by Pam Poll

First edition
Published by Geneva Press
Louisville, Kentucky

This book is printed on acid free paper that meets the American National Standards Institute Z39.48 standard. ∞

PRINTED IN THE UNITED STATES OF AMERICA
99 00 01 02 03 04 05 06 07 08 — 10 9 8 7 6 5 4 3 2 1

ISBN 0-664-50030-7 (Leader's Edition)
ISBN 0-664-50029-3 (Presbyterian Pew Edition)
ISBN 0-664-50144-3 (Ecumenical Pew Edition)

Contents

Foreword

*Let us lift up our hearts as well
as our hands
to God in heaven.*
Lam. 3:41

Lift Up Your Hearts, a collection of contemporary songs and hymns for use in Christian worship, appears at a time of great flux in the life and liturgy of the church. People today are hungry for experiences of the holy, but established patterns of church attendance, Christian education, and liturgical practice are undergoing great change. People come to churches seeking spiritual meaning and depth, but they often have little acquaintance with the church's vocabulary, the biblical story, the great hymns of the tradition, and the classical language of worship.

In response to this new cultural climate, many congregations have been experimenting with newer styles of worship, including contemporary music that is easy to learn and to sing. Sometimes tensions have arisen in congregations as older, more traditional worship forms jostled with the newer, less formal styles. As more and more churches have adapted their worship patterns, the need has arisen for a collection of songs and hymns that would, on the other hand, embody the strong theology and musical excellence vital to trustworthy Christian liturgy. *Lift Up Your Hearts* is addressed to this need.

The committee that assembled the collection of songs in *Lift Up Your Hearts* has sought, in every case, to find music that faithfully expresses the convictions of the Reformed theological tradition. A wide variety of contemporary Christian music was surveyed in order to select the best songs for this collection. Whenever possible and needed, changes have been made in the language of the songs to render them inclusive in regard to language about human beings. All of the music is easy to sing, but not simplistic or overly sentimental.

There are two versions of *Lift Up Your Hearts:* the Leader's Edition and the Pew Edition. The Leader's Edition is a large-format book featuring written-out accompaniment for all songs, including parts for various instruments where suitable, as well as suggestions for tempo and interpretation. The Pew Edition is a smaller, easy-to-hold book, which includes the words, melody line, and guitar chords of the songs. This edition is available in two different bindings, designated Presbyterian Pew Edition and Ecumenical Pew Edition.

We hope that these songs will bless you and your congregation as they have blessed those of us who have assembled this collection. Our prayer is that, as you sing these songs, you will truly be encouraged to "lift up your hearts" to God.

Linda White, Editor

As We Gather in This Place

Gathering

Words and music by
Kevin Boyd

As we gath-er in this place   We have come to seek your face.   May our lives re-flect your grace   As we gath-er in this place.

Blessed Are Those

Ps. 84
Gathering

Words and Music by
Burns Stanfield

Bless - ed are those who dwell in your house,   Ev - er sing-ing your praise.   Bless - ed are those who dwell in your house,   Ev - er sing - ing your praise.

1. AS WE GATHER IN THIS PLACE   2. BLESSED ARE THOSE

City of God

Isa. 40:1–9
Gathering

Words and Music by
Dan Schutte

1. A - wake from your slum - ber!
2. We are sons of the morn - ing;
3. O ___ com - fort my peo - ple;

A - rise from your sleep!
we are daugh-ters of day.
make gen - tle your words.

A new day is
The one who has
Pro-claim to my

dawn - ing
loved us
cit - y

for all those who weep.
has bright-ened our way.
the day of her birth.

The peo - ple in dark - ness
The Lord of all kind - ness
O cit - y of glad - ness,

have seen a great
has called us to
now lift up your

Light.
be
voice.

The Lord of our long - ing
A light for his peo - ple
Pro - claim the good tid - ings

has con-quered the night.
to set their hearts free.
that all may re - joice.

Let us

3. CITY OF GOD

build the cit-y of God. May our tears be turned in-to danc-

- ing! For the Lord, our light and our love, has turned the

night in-to day! day! Let us day!

Come and Fill

Gathering

Words and Music by
The Taizé Community

Come and fill our hearts with your peace.

You a-lone, O Lord, are ho-ly. Come and fill our hearts

with your peace, al-le-lu - ia!

4. COME AND FILL

Family Song

John 3:31–35
Gathering/Community

Words and Music by
Steve Hampton

Here we are, gath - ered to - geth-
(sing - ing)

- er as a fam - i - ly;

Bound as one, lift - ing up our voic - es to the

King of kings. We cry, "Ab - ba,
(We sing,)

Fa - ther, wor - thy is your name.
(ho - ly)

Ab - ba, Fa - ther, wor-thy is your name."
(ho - ly)

5. **FAMILY SONG**

I Was Glad

Ps. 122:1
Gathering

Words and Music by
Kinley Lange

6. I WAS GLAD

I Will Call upon the Lord

Ps. 18:3, 46
Gathering

Words and Music by
Michael O'Shields

I will call up-on the Lord

who is wor-thy to be praised.

So shall I be saved from my en-e-mies. _____

I will call up-on the Lord. Lord. The

Lord liv-eth, and bless-ed be the Rock. And let the God

of my sal-va-tion be ex-alt-ed. The Lord liv-eth, and

7. I WILL CALL UPON THE LORD

bless - ed be the Rock, and let the God __ of my sal -

va-tion be ex - alt - ed. The ed.

Optional Descant

Verse

I will call up-on the Lord

who is wor - thy to be praised.

So shall I be saved from my en - e - mies.

Second time to Chorus

I will call up - on the Lord.

Come into His Presence

Rom. 10:9; Rev. 5:12
Gathering

Composer/Lyricist: Unknown

1. Come in - to his pres-ence sing-ing Al - le - lu -
2. Come in - to his pres-ence sing-ing Je - sus is
3. Praise the Lord to - geth - er sing-ing Wor - thy the
4. Praise the Lord to - geth - er sing-ing Glo - ry to

ia, al - le - lu - ia, al - le - lu - ia.
Lord, Je - sus is Lord, Je - sus is Lord.
Lamb, wor - thy the Lamb, wor - thy the Lamb.
God, glo - ry to God, glo - ry to God.

Come in - to his pres - ence sing - ing Al - le - lu -
Come in - to his pres - ence sing - ing Je - sus is
Praise the Lord to - geth - er sing - ing Wor - thy the
Praise the Lord to - geth - er sing - ing Glo - ry to

Last time, repeat as necessary

ia, al - le - lu - ia, al - le - lu - ia.
Lord, Je - sus is Lord, Je - sus is Lord.
Lamb, wor - thy the Lamb, wor - thy the Lamb.
God, glo - ry to God, glo - ry to God.

Jesus, We Are Here

Gathering

Words and Music by
Patrick Matsikenyiri

Je - sus, we are here, Je - sus,
Je - su ta - wa pa - no, Je - su

we are here, Je - sus, we are here,
ta - wa pa - no, Je - su ta - wa pa - no,

we are here _____ for _____ you.
ta - wa pa - no mu zi - ta re

Mam-bo Je - su nyu. _____

Let Us Go!

Ps. 100:2, 4; Ps. 122:1
Call to Worship

Words and Music by
Walt Harrah

1. I re - joiced with those who said to me,
(2. We have) come to lis - ten to the Word,
(3. He will) meet us as we seek his face,

"Let us go to the house of the Lord."
There's no
Here the
And he

oth - er place I'd rath - er be,
Spir - it's pres-ence is as-sured. Let us go to the house of the Lord.
chang-es peo - ple in this place.

Gath-ered here with all God's fam - i - ly,
Je - sus Christ will be ex - alt - ed here, Let us
With a grate-ful heart we've come to sing,

go to the house of the Lord.
Who could ask for bet - ter
As the one we wor-ship
Giv - ing thanks to God in

com - pa - ny?
and re - vere. Let us go to the house of the Lord.
ev - ery-thing.

10. LET US GO!

Enter in - to his gates with praise, Thank the Lord Most High.

— Enter in - to his courts with joy,

1., 2.

praise and glo - ri - fy. _____

3.

G2 A A

2. We have
3. He will

And glo - ri - fy. _____   And glo - ri - fy!

10. LET US GO!

Make a Joyful Noise

Ps. 100
Gathering

Words and Music by
Kinley Lange

Make a joy - ful noise un - to the Lord, all peo - ple make a joy - ful noise. ___

Make a joy - ful noise un - to the Lord, all

peo - ple make a joy - ful noise. ___

Serve the Lord with glad - ness, come in -

to God's pres-ence with a song. Serve the Lord with

11. **MAKE A JOYFUL NOISE**

glad-ness, come in - to God's pres-ence with a song. Make a

peo - ple make a joy - ful noise! __

Make a Joyful Noise All the Earth

Ps. 100
Gathering

Words and Music by
Linnea Good

Make a joy-ful noise all the earth!

Wor-ship your God with glad-ness. Make a joy-ful noise all the earth.

Come to this place with a song!

Verses

1. Know that your God has made you.
2. En - ter these gates, thanks giv - ing.
3. A - ges through end - less a - ges,

Know it's to God we be - long. And
En - ter these courts ____ with praise. Sing
sea - sons of end - less years, the

come to this place with joy - ful-ness and praise.
thanks to your God and bless this ho - ly name.
love of our ma - ker ev - er shall en - dure.

Wor - ship your God with a song!

12. MAKE A JOYFUL NOISE ALL THE EARTH

Spirit Song

Col. 1:9–13
Gathering/Jesus the Son

Words and Music by
John Wimber

1. O let the Son of God en-fold you with his
2. O come and sing this song with glad-ness as your

Spir-it and his love, Let him fill your life and
hearts are filled with joy, Lift your hands in sweet sur-

sat-is-fy your soul. O let him
ren-der to his name. O give him

have the things that hold you and his Spir-it, like a
all your tears and sad-ness, give him all your years of

dove, Will des-cend up-on your life and make you
pain, And you'll en-ter in-to life in Je-sus'

whole. Je - sus, O Je - sus,
name.

come and fill your lambs. Je - sus, O

Je - sus, come and fill your lambs.

13. SPIRIT SONG

Over My Head

Traditional

1. O-ver my head   I hear mu-sic in the air.
(2. O-ver my) head   I hear sing-ing in the air.

O-ver my head   I hear mu-sic in the air.
O-ver my head   I hear sing-ing in the air.

O-ver my head   I hear mu-sic in the air.
O-ver my head   I hear sing-ing in the air.

There must be   a God some-where.   2. O-ver my
There must be   a God some-

where.   There must be   a God some-where.

This Is the Day

Ps. 118:24
Gathering

Words and Music by
Bobby Fisher

This is the day, ___ This is

the day, ___ This is the day ___ that the

Lord has made! Let us re-joice,

Let us re-joice, ___ Let us re-joice

___ and be glad!

Let us re-joice ___ and be glad! ___

15. THIS IS THE DAY

We Are the Family of God

Eph. 3:14–21
Gathering/Community

Words and Music by
Jon Byron

16.   WE ARE THE FAMILY OF GOD

You Oh Lord Are a Great God

Heb. 13:15
Gathering

Words and Music by
Terry and Randy Butler

1. I come to you oh Lord _ with a
(2. I) bring to you oh Lord _ a

thank - ful heart. I sing my song of love _
sac - ri - fice of praise. _ And of your won-drous works,

and praise for who you are. _____
I'll sing for all my days. _____

For you oh Lord are a great God,

glo - ri - ous and strong. You oh Lord are a great

Am   C   D7sus   G
_____ God, I wor-ship you a - lone.   2. I

For you oh Lord are a great _ God,

glo - ri - ous and strong. You oh Lord are a great

_ God, I wor-ship you a - lone. I

come to you oh Lord _ with a thank - ful heart.

17. YOU OH LORD ARE A GREAT GOD

You Are Here

Gathering

Words and Music by
Martin J. Nystrom and Don Moen

You are here __ a - mong us,

for we have gath - ered in your name. We can feel

your pres - ence in this place. __

You are here __ a - mong us. You are en -

throned up - on our praise. You are here, here to heal

_ and here to save. __ You are here

18. YOU ARE HERE

in our midst, how we've wait - ed for mo-

- ments like this. __ Have your way __ in this place,

__ Ho - ly Spir - it, come do as you wish.

__ We are changed as you move in our midst.

18. YOU ARE HERE

Alleluia!

Songs of Praise

Words and Music by
Michael McCarty

Al - le, al - le - lu - ia!

Al - le, al - le - lu - ia! Al - le,

al - le - lu - ia! Al - le, al - le - lu - ia!

19. ALLELUIA! (McCarty)

Alleluia

Songs of Praise

Words and Music by
Jerry Sinclair

20. ALLELUIA (Sinclair)

Alleluia, Thanks Be to God

Songs of Praise

Words and Music by
Jim Strathdee

Al - le - lu - ia, al - le - lu - ia, al - le - lu - ia, thanks be to God.

Descant—second time

Al - le - lu - ia, al - le - lu - ia, al - le - lu - ia, thanks be to God.

21.   ALLELUIA, THANKS BE TO GOD

Blessed Be the Lord God Almighty

Rev. 4:8

Songs of Praise/Response to Pardon

Words and Music by
Bob Fitts

Fa-ther in heav-en, how we love you, we

lift your name in all the earth. May your

king - dom be es-tab-lished in our prais - es,

as your peo - ple de - clare your might - y works.

Bless-ed be the Lord God Al - might - y, who

was, and is, and is to come; Bless-ed be the

22. BLESSED BE THE LORD GOD ALMIGHTY

22. **BLESSED BE THE LORD GOD ALMIGHTY**

Awesome God

Ps. 145:1–9; James 3:17
Songs of Praise

Words and music by
Rich Mullins

Our God is an awe-some God,

he reigns from heav-en a-bove with

wis-dom, pow'r and love. Our God is an awe-some

God! Our God! Our God is an awe-some

God! Our God is an awe-some God!

23. **AWESOME GOD**

God Is So Good

2 Chron. 5:11–14
Songs of Praise

Words and Music: Unknown

1. God is so good,
2. God an - swers prayer,
3. God cares for me,
4. God, you're so good,

God is so good, God is so
God an - swers prayer, God an - swers
God cares for me, God cares for
God, you're so good, God, you're so

good, God is good to me.
prayer, God is good to me.
me, God is good to me.
good, you're so good to

me, you're so good to me.

From the Sun's Rising

Matt. 28:16
Songs of Praise

Words and music by
Graham Kendrick

1. From the sun's ris - ing un - to the sun's
2. To ev - 'ry tongue, tribe, and na - tion he
3. Come let us join with the church from all

set - ting, Je - sus our Lord shall be
sends us, to make dis - ci - ples, to
na - tions, cross ev - 'ry bor - der, throw

great in the earth; and all earth's king - doms shall
teach, and bap - tize. For all au - thor - i - ty
wide ev - 'ry door; Work - ers with him as he

be his do - min - ion, all of cre - a - tion shall
to him is giv - en; Now as his wit - ness - es
gath - ers his har - vest, till earth's far cor - ners our

sing of his worth. _____
we shall a - rise. _____
Sav - ior a - dore. _____

25. FROM THE SUN'S RISING

25. **FROM THE SUN'S RISING**

Blessed Be Your Holy Name

Songs of Praise

Words and Music by
Eddie Espinosa

26. **BLESSED BE YOUR HOLY NAME**

26. **BLESSED BE YOUR HOLY NAME**

God the Creator

Psalm 37:5
Songs of Praise

Gaelic melody
Words and arrangement by
The Iona Community

1. God the Cre - a - tor, you in love made me,
2. O Christ the Sav - ior, you in love called me,

who once was noth - ing, but now have grown.
who once was no one, lost and a - lone.

I bring the best of all my life of - fers;
I pledge to go wher - ev - er you sum - mon,

for you I share what - ev - er I own.
mak-ing your will and pur-pose my

own.   3. O God the spir - it, you in love
                                             peo - ple sum-moned to -

move   me,   who once was   no - where   and   felt   un -
geth - er   to   be   the   Church   in   which faith is

known.   I know my   need   of   you   for com -
sown.   I make my   prom - ise   to   live   for

pan - ion: all things can change when   not   on   my
Je - sus   and   let   the   world know   all   are   his

own.   4. And with the   own.

Halle, Halle, Hallelujah

Songs of Praise

Music: Unknown
Arr. Geoff Weaver

Music arrangement © 1993 Geoff Weaver/Jubilate Hymns.
Used by permission of G.I.A. Publications, Inc.

28. HALLE, HALLE, HALLELUJAH

Great and Mighty

Ps. 150
Songs of Praise

Words and Music by
Marlene Bigley

29. GREAT AND MIGHTY

Great Is the Lord

Songs of Praise

Words and Music by
Michael W. Smith and Deborah D. Smith

1. Great is the Lord, he is ho - ly and just.
2. Great are you, Lord, You are ho - ly and just:

By his pow - er we trust in his love.
By your po - wer we trust in your love.

Great is the Lord, he is faith - ful and true;
Great are you, Lord, you are faith - ful and true;

By his mer - cy he proves he is love.
By your mer - cy you prove you are love.

Great is the Lord, and wor - thy of glo - ry!
Great are you, Lord, and wor - thy of glo - ry!

Great is the Lord and wor - thy of praise.
Great are you, Lord, and wor - thy of praise.

30. GREAT IS THE LORD

Great   is   the   Lord;   now   lift   up   your   voice,   Now
Great   are   you,   Lord;   I   lift   up   my   voice,   I

lift   up   your   voice: Great _____ is   the
lift   up   my   voice: Great _____ are   you,

Lord! _____ Great _____ is   the
Lord! _____ Great _____ are   you,

Lord! _____
Lord! _____

30.   GREAT IS THE LORD

Holy Is the Lord on High

Songs of Praise

Words and Music by
Scott Brenner

In the still - ness of this hour

I wor - ship you, my Lord, __ cry - ing,

"Ho - ly is ____ the Lord on high."

In the qui - et of my heart __

I sing this song of praise, cry - ing,

"Ho - ly is ____ the Lord on high."

31. HOLY IS THE LORD ON HIGH

And   for   all   of   my   days _____   I   will

bow   down   be - fore _____   you,   giv-ing   glo - ry   and   hon -

- or   to   your   name.   And   for

all   of   my   life _____   I   will   wor - ship   and   a - dore

_____   you,   cry-ing,   "Ho - ly   is _____   the   Lord   on

high."   In   the   still -   cry - ing,

"Ho - ly   is _____   the   Lord   on   high."

31. HOLY IS THE LORD ON HIGH

Holy Lord

Isa. 6:3
Songs of Praise

Words and Music by
Claire Cloninger and Don Moen

1. We hear your voice as a sound of wings,
2. In your light we are filled with light —

— we see your glo-ry as a cloud; We feel your
— as we be-hold you face to face; The words of

pres-ence as our hearts draw near, as be-fore your ho-li-
earth and heav-en rise — to you in a per-fect of-fer-

ness we bow. _____ Ho-ly Lord, —
ing of praise. _____

clothed in maj-es-ty and won-der; _____ ho-ly

God, it is you — that we a-dore; _____

32. HOLY LORD

Tribes and tongues raise a song ___ like ho - ly thun - der, _____ sing - ing, "Ho - ly, ho - ly, ho -

- ly is the Lord." _____ Sing - ing

"Ho - ly, ho - ly, ho - ly is the Lord. __

He Is Exalted

Songs of Praise/Christ the King/Transfiguration

Words and Music by
Twila Paris

33. HE IS EXALTED

How Can I Keep from Singing?

Ps. 30:5
Songs of Praise

Words and Music by Robert Lowry,
Bright Jewels for the Sunday School, 1869
Refrain music alt.

1. My life flows on in end - less song,
2. Through all the tu - mult and the strife,
3. What though my joys and com - forts die?
4. The peace of Christ makes fresh my heart,

a - bove earth's lam - en - ta - tion. I
I hear that mus - ic ring - ing. It
The Lord my Sav - ior liv - eth. What
a foun - tain ev - er spring - ing! All

catch the sweet, though far - off hymn that
finds an ech - o in my soul. How
though the dark - ness gath - er round? Songs
things are mine since I am his! How

hails a new cre - a - tion.
can I keep from sing - ing?   No storm can shake my
in the night he giv - eth.
can I keep from sing - ing?

in - most calm while to that Rock I'm cling - ing. Since

love is Lord of heav'n and earth, how can I keep from sing - ing?

34. HOW CAN I KEEP FROM SINGING?

I Sing Praises

Songs of Praise

Words and Music by
Terry MacAlmon

1. I sing prais-es to your name, O Lord, prais-es to your name, O Lord, for your name is great and great-ly to be praised.
2. I give glo-ry to your name, O Lord, glo-ry to your name, O Lord, for your name is great and great-ly to be praised.

I sing prais-es to your name, O Lord, prais-es to your name, O Lord, for your name is great and great-ly to be praised.
I give glo-ry to your name, O Lord, glo-ry to your name, O Lord, for your name is great and great-ly to be praised.

35. I SING PRAISES

I Will Sing of the Mercies

Songs of Praise

Words and Music by
John Barnett

In the Presence of Your People

Ps. 22:3,22; Ps. 116:14
Response to Pardon/Songs of Praise

Words para. by Brent Chambers
Music by Brent Chambers

37. IN THE PRESENCE OF YOUR PEOPLE

good - ness   and   your   stead-fast love;   May   your

name be ex - alt - ed   here   on   earth and in   heav'n a - bove.

37.   **IN THE PRESENCE OF YOUR PEOPLE**

I Will Worship You, Lord

Ps. 72:19
Songs of Praise

Words and Music by
Daniel Gardner

38. I WILL WORSHIP YOU, LORD

May my heart be pure and ho-ly in thy sight as I
wor-ship you with all of my might.

Jesus, Name above All Names

John 1:1–14
Songs of Praise/Advent

Words and Music by
Naida Hearn

Je - sus, name a - bove all names;
beau - ti - ful Sav - ior, glo - ri - ous
Lord. _____ Em - man - u - el,
God is with us; bless - ed Re -
deem - er, Liv - ing Word. _____

39. JESUS, NAME ABOVE ALL NAMES

Jesus, You're the Way

John 14:6
Songs of Praise

Words and Music by
Walt Harrah

1. Je - sus, you're the way. __ In you all
2. Je - sus, Prince of Peace, the Branch from
3. Shep - herd of the soul, __ the light of

truth is found, The foun - tain - head of life, __
Da - vid's throne, Mes - si - ah Son of God,
ev - 'ry - one, __ the King of Kings who reigns

__ the on - ly door: _____
__ the Great I Am: _____
__ in glo - ry now: _____

Where else can I turn? _ Where else can I go?

__ You a - lone have the on - ly words I

40. JESUS, YOU'RE THE WAY

need to know.

You a - lone have the

on - ly words I need to know. ___

40. JESUS, YOU'RE THE WAY

Let There Be Praise

Songs of Praise

Words and Music by
Melodie and Dick Tunney

1., 2. Let there be praise, let there be

joy in our hearts. Sing to ___
For - ev -

___ the Lord, give him the glo - ry; ___
- er - more let his love

___ fill the air, and

let there be praise.

Let there be praise, let there be

41. LET THERE BE PRAISE

41.   LET THERE BE PRAISE

Lord of All

Songs of Praise

Words and Music by
Danny Daniels

You are   Lord   o - ver   night __   and   day.

You are   Lord and the one __ who   saves.   You are   Lord and we sing

__ your   praise.   You are   Lord   of   all. ____

You are   Lord   of the   winds   that   blow.   You are   Lord   in the love

__ you   show.   You are   Lord; let the peo - ple   know

You are   Lord   of   all! ____   You   are   Lord

__ of the heav - ens.   You   are   Lord __ of the na - tions.

42. LORD OF ALL

1.
G D Em   C   D
You are Lord, — you are Lord of all. —

2.
G D Em   C D G
You are Lord, — you are Lord of all!

Lord, Be Glorified

Songs of Praise

Words and Music by
Bob Kilpatrick

C   G   Am   Em7   Dm7   G
In   my   life, Lord,   be   glo - ri - fied,
In   your   church, Lord,   be   glo - ri - fied,

B♭   G7   C   G/B   Am   Em
be   glo - ri - fied.   In   my   life,   Lord,
be   glo - ri - fied.   In   your   church,   Lord,

Dm7   G   C   F/A G7/B   C   Fine
be   glo - ri - fied   to - day.
be   glo - ri - fied   to - day.

43.   LORD, BE GLORIFIED

Lord, Glorify Your Name

Songs of Praise

Words and Music by
Robert Hartmann

44. LORD, GLORIFY YOUR NAME

Lord, You Are the Holy One

Songs of Praise

Words and Music by
Lynn DeShazo

Lord, you are the Ho - ly One, and by your grace we come to sing this song to you, we de-light our-selves in you; For - ev - er you're the same, we mag-ni-fy your name, and of your deeds we tell, Ho - ly One of Is - ra - el. Lord, you are Ho - ly, ho - ly. And you are wor - thy to be praised; Fa - ther, we love you, love you. There is no oth - er who shall reign.

45. LORD, YOU ARE THE HOLY ONE

Majesty

Songs of Praise/Easter/Ascension/Christ the King

Words and Music by
Jack W. Hayford

Maj - es - ty, _____ wor-ship his maj - es - ty; _____

_____ un - to Je - sus be all glo - ry, hon-or and

praise. _____ Maj - es - ty, _____ king-dom au-

thor - i - ty _____ flow from his throne un - to his

own, his an - them raise. _____ So ex -

alt, lift up on high the name of Je - sus; _____

46. MAJESTY

Santo, Santo

Songs of Praise

Words and Music: Unknown

1. San - to, san - to, san - to, mi
2. Ho - ly, ho - ly, ho - ly, my

co - ra - zón te_a - do - ra! Mi co - ra - zón te
heart, my heart a - dores you! My heart is glad to

sa - be de - cir: San - to_e - res, Se - ñor.
say ____ the words: You are ho - ly,

Lord. You are ho - ly, Lord.

47. SANTO, SANTO

Praise, I Will Praise You, Lord

Ps. 145
Songs of Praise

Words and Music by
Claude Fraysse

1. Praise, I will praise you, Lord,
2. Love, I will love you, Lord, with
3. Serve, I will serve you, Lord,

all my heart. O God, I will tell the

won-ders of your ways, and glo-ri-fy your name.

Praise, I will praise you, Lord,
Love, I will love you, Lord, with all my
Serve, I will serve you, Lord

heart. In you I will find the source of all my joy.

1., 2.
Al - le - lu - ia!

3.
le - lu - ia!

48. PRAISE, I WILL PRAISE YOU, LORD

Mighty Is Our God

Ps. 93:4
Songs of Praise

Words and Music by
Don Moen, Eugene Greco, and Gerrit Gustafson

Might-y is our God, might-y is our King;

Might-y is our Lord, __

rul-er of ev-'ry-thing. Glor-y to our God,

__ glo-ry to our King; __

Glo-ry to our Lord, rul-er of ev-'ry-thing.

His name is high-er, high-er than an-y oth-

49. MIGHTY IS OUR GOD

49. **MIGHTY IS OUR GOD**

Shine, Jesus, Shine

Songs of Praise

Words and Music by
Graham Kendrick

1. Lord, the light of your love is shin - ing
2. Lord, I come to your awe - some pres - ence,
3. As we gaze on your king - ly bright - ness,

in the midst of the dark - ness, shin - ing;
from the shad - ows in - to your ra - dience;
so our fa - ces dis - play your like - ness,

Je - sus, Light of the World, shine up - on us,
by the blood I may en - ter your bright - ness,
ev - er chang - ing from glo - ry to glo - ry,

set us free by the truth you now bring - us:
search me, try me, con - sume all my dark - ness:
mir - rored here may our lives tell your sto - ry:

Shine on me, shine on me.

50. SHINE, JESUS, SHINE

Shine, Je - sus, shine, — fill this land with the

Fa - ther's glo - ry. Blaze, Spir - it, blaze, set our

hearts on fire. Flow, riv - er, flow,

— flood the na - tions with grace and mer - cy.

Send forth your word, — Lord, and let there be

light! _____ light!

light! _____

50. SHINE, JESUS, SHINE

The Name of the Lord

Prov. 18:10
Songs of Praise

Music by
Clinton Utterbach

51. THE NAME OF THE LORD

51. THE NAME OF THE LORD

Sing Hallelujah

Songs of Praise

Words and Music by
Linda Stassen

52. SING HALLELUJAH

Sing unto the Lord

Ps. 96:1, 4
Songs of Praise/Call to Worship/Psalm Refrain

Words and Music: Unknown
Arr. by Tom Fettke

Arr. Tom Fettke/Word Music/ASCAP
Arr. © 1992 Word Music, Inc. All Rights Reserved. Used by permission.

53. SING UNTO THE LORD

Thou Art Worthy

Rev. 4:11
Songs of Praise

Words and Music by
Pauline Michael Mills

54. THOU ART WORTHY

We Will Glorify

Songs of Praise

Words and Music by
Twila Paris

1. We will glo - ri - fy the King of kings, we will
2. Lord Je - ho - vah reigns in maj - es - ty, we will
3. He is Lord of heav - en, Lord of earth, he is
4. Hal - le - lu - jah to the King of kings, hal - le -

glo - ri - fy the Lamb; We will glo - ri - fy the
bow be - fore his throne; We will wor - ship him in
Lord of all who live; He is Lord a - bove the
lu - jah to the Lamb; Hal - le - lu - jah to the

Lord of lords, who __ is the great I AM.
right-eous-ness, we will wor - ship him a - lone.
u - ni - verse, all __ praise to him we give.
Lord of lords, who __ is the great I AM.

55. WE WILL GLORIFY

We Are Singing

Ps. 27:1–4; 96:1, 4; Col. 3:16
Songs of Praise

Zulu text and music based on the
South African freedom song "Siyahamba."
Free paraphrase of Zulu text in English, additional text,
and music arrangement by Hal H. Hopson

Refrain

We are sing - ing, for the Lord is our light,
See yah hahm buh koo kah nigh nee kwen kohs,

We are sing - ing, for the Lord is our light. ___
see yah hahm buh koo kah nigh nee kwen kohs. ___

We are sing - ing, for the Lord is our light,
See yah hahm buh koo kah nigh nee kwen kohs,

We are sing - ing, for the Lord is our light. ___
see yah hahm buh koo kah nigh nee kwen kohs. ___

We are sing - ing, _____ Oh, we are sing - ing,
See yah hahm buh, _____ Oh, see yah hahm buh

for the Lord is our light. __ We are sing - ing, _____
koo kah nigh nee kwen kohs. __ *See yah hahm buh,* _____

Oh, we are sing - ing, for the Lord is our light. __
Oh, see yah hahm buh koo kah nigh nee kwen kohs. __

Verses

1. The Lord is the strength of our lives; __
2. One thing have we asked of the Lord, __
3. When bur - dens are heav - y to bear, __
4. We walk in the strength of the Lord, __

of whom shall we be a - fraid? __ Though
yes, this is the thing we seek: __ To
our shel - ter is God a - lone. __ Our
God's love ____ is ev - er sure. __ We

foes may be near to de - stroy; __ the
dwell in the house of the Lord; __ to
feet are ___ lift - ed high; __ yes,
shout that the world may hear, __ we

Lord will be our light. _____
live with God for - ev - er. _____
high up - on a rock. _____
sing a joy - ful song. _____

56. WE ARE SINGING

We Bow Down

Songs of Praise

Words and Music by
Twila Paris

You are Lord of cre - a - tion and

Lord of my life, Lord of the land __ and the sea.

You were Lord of the heav - ens be - fore there was

time, And Lord of all lords you will be! We bow

down ____ and we wor - ship you, Lord. We bow

down ____ and we wor - ship you, Lord. We bow

57. WE BOW DOWN

down ____ and we wor - ship you, Lord,

Lord of all lords you will be!

You are

I Bow Down

Songs of Praise

Words and Music by
Walt Harrah

58. I BOW DOWN

We Bring the Sacrifice of Praise

Ps. 116:17; Heb. 13:15
Songs of Praise

Words and Music by
Kirk Dearman

We bring the sac - ri - fice of praise in - to the

house of the Lord; We bring the sac - ri - fice of

praise in - to the house of the Lord. And we

of - fer up to you the sac - ri - fic - es of

thanks - giv - ing; And we of - fer up to you

Bm7   Em7   A7   1. D   G/A   2. D

the sac - ri - fic - es of joy!   joy!

59. WE BRING THE SACRIFICE OF PRAISE

With My Whole Heart

Zeph. 3:14
Songs of Praise

Words and Music by
Danny Chambers

With my whole heart, I will re-joice, with a

new song, make a joy - ful noise; Might-y

Sav - ior, I will bless your name, you have

saved me from a life of shame. To the

God of my sal - va - tion I make this dec - la - ra - tion,

"You a - lone are the Lord of all.

60. WITH MY WHOLE HEART

You a-lone are the Lord of all.

Je-sus Christ is the Lord of all.

Je-sus Christ is the Lord of all.

Je-sus Christ is the Lord of all."

60. WITH MY WHOLE HEART

Change My Heart, O God

Isa. 64:8
Confession

Words and music by
Eddie Espinosa

Change my heart, O God, Make it ev-er true.

Change my heart, O God, May I be like you.

You are the pot - ter, I am the clay, —

Mold me and make me, This is what I pray.

Change my heart, O God, Make it ev-er true. —

Change my heart, O God, — May I be like you.

61. CHANGE MY HEART, O GOD

Kyrie Eleison

Confession

Words: Ancient Greek liturgy
Music: Russian Orthodox liturgy

Ky - ri - e e - lei - son. Ky - ri - e e -

lei - son. Ky - ri - e e - le - i - son.

Lord, Have Mercy

Confession

Words and music by
Jim Strathdee

Lord, have mer - cy. Christ, have mer - cy.

Lord, have mer - cy up - on us.

Come to Me

Matt. 11:28–30
Confession

Music by
Walt Harrah

heart. _____ And you will find rest,
rest for your soul, for my yoke is eas-
-y and my bur - den is light. _____
rest, _____ and I _____ will give you rest. _____

64.   COME TO ME

Kind and Merciful God

Confession

Words by Bryan Jeffrey Leech, 1973
Music: Traditional Swedish melody;
adapt. Bryan Jeffrey Leech, 1973

1. Kind and mer - ci - ful God, we have
2. Kind and mer - ci - ful God, we've ne -
3. Kind and mer - ci - ful God, we have
4. Kind and mer - ci - ful God, in Christ's
5. Kind and mer - ci - ful God, bid us

sinned in your sight, we have all wan - dered
glect - ed your Word and the truth that would
bro - ken your laws and in con - duct have
death on the cross you pro - vid - ed a
lift up our heads and com - mand us to

far from your way; we have fol - lowed de -
guide us a - right; we have lived in the
veered from the norm; we have dreamed of the
cleans - ing from sin; speak the words that for -
rise from our knees; may our hearts now be

65. KIND AND MERCIFUL GOD

sire,	we	have	failed	to	as - pire	to	the
shade	of	the	dark	we	have made,	when	you
good,	but	the	good	that	we could	we	have
give,	that	hence - forth	we	may	live	by	the
changed	and	no	long - er	es - tranged,	through the

vir - tue	we	ought	to	dis - play.
willed	us	to	walk	in	the	light.
fre - quent - ly	failed	to	per - form.
might	of	your	Spir - it	with - in.
pow'r	of	your	par - don	and	peace.

65. KIND AND MERCIFUL GOD

Refiner's Fire

1 John 3:1–7
Confession

Words and Music by
Brian Doerksen

There's a Place

Confession

Words and Music by
Kevin Boyd

1. There's a place of hon - es - ty and peace; Je - sus calls us. A place where bur - dens find re - lease; The Spir - it draws us.
2. There's an ad - vo - cate, a throne of grace; Je - sus calls us. A source of strength, a warm em - brace; The Spir - it draws us.
3. There's a place where wound - ed souls can mend, Je. - sus calls us. A place of mer - cy with - out end; The Spir - it draws us.

Heal - ing flood of for - give - ness, Wash a - way our ev - 'ry stain; Through the blood of our Sav - ior, Make us whole a - gain.

Rush - ing wind of God's fa - vor, fill our wan - d'ring hearts with faith; Through the blood of our Sav - ior, Make us whole a - gain.

67. THERE'S A PLACE

Healing Grace

Confession/Forgiveness

Words and music by
Gary Sadler and John Chisum

Mer - ci - ful God and Fa - ther, lov - ing us

like no oth - er, hear our prayer, the

cry of our hearts, as we come to you. We ac -

knowl-edge our trans-gres - sions, we con - fess to

you our sins; ___ show us mer - cy and com - pas -

- sion, touch our lives with your heal-ing grace a - gain.

Re - lease us from the past __ as we

seek your face: wash us clean at last. __

We re - ceive your love, we re - ceive your heal - ing

grace. We re - ceive your love, we re -

ceive your heal - ing grace. grace.

Touch our lives with your heal - ing grace a - gain.

68. HEALING GRACE

God Has Smiled on Me

Gal. 5:1, 13–25
Response to Forgiveness

Words and Music by
Isaiah Jones, Jr.

69. GOD HAS SMILED ON ME

Abundant Life

John 10:10
Response to Forgiveness

Words and Music by
Josh A. Hailey and Isaiah Jones, Jr.
Arr. by Isaiah Jones, Jr.

Bless the Lord, My Soul

Ps. 103
Response to Forgiveness

Words and Music by
The Taizé Community

Bless the Lord, my soul, and bless God's ho - ly

name. Bless the Lord, My soul, who

leads me in - to life. 1. It is life.
2. The

(1.) he who for-gives all your guilt, who heals ev - 'ry

one of your ills, who re - deems your life from the

grave, who crowns you with love and com - pas - sion.

71. BLESS THE LORD, MY SOUL

(2.) Lord is com-pas-sion and love, slow to an-ger and rich in

mer - cy. He does not treat us ac-cord-ing to our

D.C. al Fine

sins nor re - pay us ac-cord-ing to our faults.

Glory to God

Ps. 105:1–4
Response to Forgiveness

Words and Music by
Jim Strathdee

Glo - ry to God, Glo - ry to God,

praise and al - le - lu - ia. Glo - ry to God,

Glo - ry to God, praise the name of the Lord. _

72. GLORY TO GOD

Glory, Praises!

Response to Forgiveness

Words and Music by
Kevin Boyd

73. GLORY, PRAISES!

Glory, Glory, Hallelujah!

Matt. 11:28
Response to Forgiveness

Words and Music traditional

```
1. Glo - ry,    glo - ry, _____    hal - le - lu - jah!
2. I  feel  bet - ter, _____    so  much  bet - ter
3. Feel  like  shout - ing, _____  "Hal - le - lu - jah!"
```

```
Since  I   laid   my _____   bur - den   down.
Since  I   laid   my _____   bur - den   down.
Since  I   laid   my _____   bur - den   down.
```

```
Glo - ry,   glo - ry, _____   hal - le - lu - jah!
I  feel  bet - ter, _____    so  much  bet - ter
Feel  like  shout - ing, _____  "Hal - le - lu - jah!"
```

```
Since  I   laid   my   bur - den   down.
Since  I   laid   my   bur - den   down.
Since  I   laid   my   bur - den   down.
```

74.   GLORY, GLORY, HALLELUJAH!

I Will Sing of the Mercies

Ps. 89:1, 5, 8
Response to Forgiveness

Music by
James H. Fillmore

75. I WILL SING OF THE MERCIES

all gen-er - a - tions. I will sing of the mer-cies of the

Lord for - ev - er, I will sing of the mer-cies of the Lord.

Grace Greater Than Our Sin

Rom. 5:20
Response to Forgiveness

Words by Julia H. Johnston
Music by Daniel B. Towner

Grace, grace, God's grace, grace that will

par - don and cleanse with - in; Grace, grace, God's

grace, grace that is great - er than all our sin.

Justified Freely

Rom. 5:8–10
Response to Forgiveness/Justification

Music by
Walt Harrah

All have sinned, fall - en short

of the glo - ry of God, ___ of the

glo - ry of God. ___ All have sinned,

fall - en short of the glo - ry of

God. But we have been

jus - ti - fied free - ly by his grace, by the

77. JUSTIFIED FREELY

blood   of   Je - sus   Christ,

jus - ti - fied free - ly by   his   grace.

But we have been   grace.

There Is a Redeemer

Phil. 2:9
Response to Forgiveness

Words and Music by
Melody Green

1. There is a Re - deem - er, Je - sus, God's own
2. Je - sus, my Re - deem - er, Name a - bove all

Son; Pre - cious Lamb of God, Mes - si - ah,
names, Pre - cious Lamb of God, Mes - si - ah,

Ho - ly One.
Hope for sin - ners slain. Thank you, oh, my

Fa - ther, for giv-ing us your Son, and

leav - ing your Spir - it 'til the work on earth is

done.
done. 3. When I stand in

78. THERE IS A REDEEMER

glo - ry, I will see his face,

There I'll serve my King for-ev-er in that ho - ly

place. Thank you, oh, my Fa - ther, for

giv-ing us your Son, and leav - ing your

Spir - it 'til the work on earth is done and

leav - ing your Spir - it 'til the work on earth is done.

78. THERE IS A REDEEMER

Once for All

Rom. 5:1–11
Response to Forgiveness

Words and Music by
Walt Harrah

E   F#m

We have been made ho - ly,

B   E   C#m

spot-less, un - de - filed   by the blood of

F#m   B   A   E

Je - sus   once for all. ___   We have been for-

F#m   B   E   C#m

giv - en,   we've been re - con - ciled

F#m   B   A   E   **Fine**

by the blood of Je - sus   once for all. ___

D/E   E   A   Am

Once for all   there at Cal - va - ry

79. ONCE FOR ALL

Jesus died for humanity,

bearing there all our guilt and our disgrace.

Once for all by the saving blood

we've been washed in its cleansing flood.

Boldly now we approach the throne of grace.

79. ONCE FOR ALL

Oh Lord, You're Beautiful

Response to Forgiveness

Words and Music by
Keith Green

Oh Lord, you're beau - ti - ful, _____

___ your face is all I seek. _____

___ For when your eyes are on this

child, your grace a - bounds to me. _____

80. OH LORD, YOU'RE BEAUTIFUL

Surely It Is God

Isa. 12:2
Response to Forgiveness

Music by
Jack Noble White
Adapted from "The First Song of Isaiah"

Sure - ly it is God who saves me; I will

trust in him and not be a - fraid, For the

Lord is my strong-hold and my sure de - fense, and

he will be my Sav - ior.

81. SURELY IT IS GOD

Be Still and Know

Ex. 15:26; Ps. 46:10
The Word/Call to Worship/Prayer

Words: St. 1, 2 Anon.; st. 3, 4, 5 by Sylvia Washer
Music: Arr. by Lee Herrington and Tom Fettke

```
1. Be    still   and    know    that   I          am
2. I      am     the    Lord    that   heal   -   eth
3. I      nev  - er     shall   for -  sake       my
4. I'll   keep  you     in      my     per  -     fect
```

```
God.   Be    still   and    know    that   I          am
thee.  I     am      the    Lord    that   heal   -   eth
own.   I     nev  -  er     shall   for -  sake       my
peace. I'll  keep    you    in      my     per  -     fect
```

```
God.   Be    still   and    know    that   I          am
thee.  I     am      the    Lord    that   heal   -   eth
own.   I     nev  -  er     shall   for -  sake       my
peace. I'll  keep    you    in      my     per  -     fect
```

```
1., 2., 3., 4.                        5.
C2          F2   F/G      C2    C/B   Asus   A

God.                      peace.            5. The
thee.
own.
```

Arr. Tom Fettke/Word Music/ASCAP
Arr. © 1988 Word Music, Inc.
All rights reserved. Used by permission.

joy   I   give   shall   be   your   strength. The

joy   I   give   shall   be   your   strength. The

joy   I   give   shall   be   your   strength.

82.   BE STILL AND KNOW

Our God Is Mighty

Ex. 15:1–9; Matt. 28:19; Acts 2:14
The Word/Affirmation of Faith

Words and Music by
Jim Gill

83. OUR GOD IS MIGHTY

83. OUR GOD IS MIGHTY

Our God Reigns

Isa. 52:7, 53; Luke 24: 5, 6, 39
The Word

Words and Music by
Lenny Smith
Arr. by Stephen A. Beddia

1. How love - ly on the moun - tains are the
2. He had no state - ly form. He had no
3. It was our sin and guilt that bruised and
4. Meek as a lamb that's led out to the
5. Out of the tomb he came with grace and

feet of him who brings good news, _____
maj - es - ty that we should be _____
wound - ed him. It was our sin _____
slaught - er - house, dumb as a sheep _____
maj - es - ty. He is a - live! _____

good ___ news. _____ An - nounc - ing peace,
drawn to him. _____ He was de - spised,
that brought him down. _____ When we like sheep
be - fore its shearer, _____ His life ran down
He is a - live! _____ God loves us so,

84. OUR GOD REIGNS

pro - claim - ing news of hap - pi - ness: _____
and we took no ac - count of him. _____
had gone a - stray, our shep - herd came _____
up - on the ground like pour - ing rain _____
see here his hands, his feet, his side; _____

Our God reigns, _____ our God
Yet now he reigns _____ with the most
And on his shoul - ders bore our
That we might be _____ born a -
Yes, we know _____ he is a -

reigns! _____
high! _____
shame! _____ Our God reigns, _____
gain! _____
live! _____

our God reigns, _____ our God reigns, _____

_____ our God reigns! Our God

84. OUR GOD REIGNS

Thy Word

Ps. 119:105
The Word/Prayer/Affirmation of Faith

Words by Amy Grant
Music by Michael W. Smith

85. THY WORD

Please be near me to the end. _____

Thy Word is a lamp un-to my feet and a

light un - to my path.

Thy Word is a lamp un-to my feet and a

light un - to my path. Thy Word is a

lamp un-to my feet and a light un-to my path.

85. **THY WORD**

She Flies On!

Gen. 1:2; Joel 2:8–29; Luke 1:35–38; Acts 2:2–8
The Word/Pentecost/Advent/Christmas

Words and Music by
Gordon Light
Arr. by Darryl Nixon

She comes sail - ing on the wind, her wings

flash - ing in the sun; on a jour - ney just be -

gun, she flies on. _____ And in the

pas - sage of her flight, her song rings out through the

night, full of laugh-ter, full of light, she flies on.

1. Si - lent wa - ters rock - ing ____ on the
2. Man - y were the dream-ers ____ whose
3. To a gen - tle girl in Gal - i - lee a ____

86. SHE FLIES ON!

G   G7   C   F

morn - ing of our   birth, like an   emp - ty   cra - dle
eyes were giv - en   sight, when the   Spir - it   filled their
gen - tle breeze she   came, ___ a   whis - per soft - ly

C/E   F   Gsus   G   Em

wait - ing to be   filled. ___   And   from the heart of
dreams with life and form. ___   Des - erts turned to
call - ing in the   dark, ___   The   prom-ise of a

Am   G   G7   C

God   the Spir - it moved up - on the earth, like   a
gar - dens, brok - en hearts found new de - light, and then
child of peace whose reign would nev - er   end, Mar - y

F   C/E   F   Am   Dm7/F   G

moth - er breath-ing life in - to her   child. ___
down the a - ges still ___ she flew on. ___
sang the Spir - it song with - in her heart. ___

86. SHE FLIES ON!

On Eagles' Wings

Ex. 19:4; Ps. 17:8; 91:1–6, 14–16
The Word/Psalm/Affirmation of Faith/Funeral

Words and music by
Michael Joncas

And he will raise you up on ea - gles' wings,

bear you on the breath of dawn, make you to shine like the

Last time continue

sun, and hold you in the palm of his hand.

And hold you, hold you in the

palm _____ of his hand. _____

87. ON EAGLES' WINGS

In the Bulb There Is a Flower

John 11:17–44; 1 Cor. 15:51–54a; 2 Cor. 5:16–21
Response to the Word

Words and Music by
Natalie Sleeth

88. IN THE BULB THERE IS A FLOWER

Here I Stand

Luke 11:9; Rev. 3:20
Response to the Word/Communion

Words and Music by
The Iona Community

Here I stand at the door _____ and knock, ___
Here I stand at the door and

___ and knock. I will come and dine _____
knock, and knock. I will dine with

___ with those who ask me in.
those who ask me in.

I Believe in Jesus

Response to the Word

Words and Music by
Marc Nelson

I be-lieve in Je - sus, I be-lieve he
(you, Lord,) (you

89. HERE I STAND   **90. I BELIEVE IN JESUS**

90. I BELIEVE IN JESUS

Let Me Have My Way among You

Col. 3:15; Heb. 4:6–11
Response to the Word

Words and Music by
Graham Kendrick

1. Let me have my way a - mong __ you, do not
2. Let my peace rule with - in your hearts, do not

strive, do not strive. Let me have my way a -
strive, do not strive. Let my peace rule with -

mong __ you, do not strive, do not strive. For
in your hearts, do not strive, do not strive. For

mine is the pow - er and the glo - ry for
mine is the pow - er and the glo - ry for

ev - er and ev - er the same. Let me
ev - er and ev - er the same. Let my

have my way a - mong you, do not strive, do not strive.
peace rule with - in your hearts, do not strive, do not strive.

91. LET ME HAVE MY WAY AMONG YOU

Lay It All Down

Phil. 3:7–10
Response to the Word/Ordination

Words and Music by
Brian Marsh

92. LAY IT ALL DOWN

Resting in You

Ps. 63:1–8
Response to the Word/Funeral/Affirmation of Faith

Words and Music by
Ed Beaty and Lenny Smith

1. In the eye of the hur - ri - cane
2. Though the moun - tains may crum-ble __
3. When my bur - dens grow heav-y ___

I find peace in __ the storm.
and the sea roll __ a - way,
and I bend be-neath the load,

Trust - ing in you, Lord, my ___ soul
know you are with me, through the night
your strength will help me down the long,

is re - born. Like a child ___ in your
and the day. For you're right ___ here in -
dust - y road. All my trials and trib - u -

arms, __ safe and warm a - gainst the night.
side me; yes, you live with - in my heart.
la - tions, they can on - ly make me strong.

93. **RESTING IN YOU**

G	G7	C

You will bear me through the dark -
I've a - ban - doned my life in -
For you lift my soul with glad -

/E	F	G7	C

ness, sur - ound - ed by your light.
to your gen - tle, lov - ing arms.
ness, and fill my heart with song.

C	/E	F	G

Rest - ing in you, Lord, safe

G7	C	C	C/E

in your arms. Rest - ing in

F	Dm	G	C

you, Lord, I am safe in your arms.

93. RESTING IN YOU

Love Is a Circle

Response to the Word

Words and Music by
Peggy Brown

1. I don't de - serve, Lord, all that I'm feel - ing,
2. I don't pre - tend to know ev - 'ry mean - ing
3. Just look a - round you. It will a - stound you.

But, Lord, I know you're real. ____ You've
of ev - 'ry - thing God does. ____
See what God's love can do. _____

giv - en me hope, you've giv - en me heal - ing,
All I can do is trust that I'm lean - ing
Let that love fill you. Now let it com - pel you to

giv - en your love as a seal _____ that
on all the won - der ____ of God's love. God's
reach out and share all it's giv - en you.

Refrain

Love is a cir - cle, the heart of all that is

real.   Love   is   a   cir - cle,   and

what   you   give you will   feel. ___

___   God's

___   And   what   you   give you will feel. ___

94. LOVE IS A CIRCLE

Sovereign Lord

Ps. 71:5–6
Response to the Word

Words and Music by
Dave Hopkins

1. For you have been my hope, O Sov - 'reign
2. For you have been our peace, O Sov - 'reign

1. For
2. For

Lord.
Lord.

For you have been my
For you have been our

you have been my hope, O Sov-'reign Lord.
you have been our peace, O Sov-'reign Lord.

hope, O Sov-'reign Lord.
peace, O Sov-'reign Lord.

O Sov-'reign
O Sov-'reign

For you have been my hope, O Sov-'reign
For you have been our peace, O Sov-'reign

95. SOVEREIGN LORD

Lord, _____ my con - fi - dence since my
Lord, _____ my con - fi - dence since my

youth. For you have been my hope, O Sov-'reign Lord.
youth. For you have been our peace, O Sov-'reign Lord.

95. **SOVEREIGN LORD**

Love the Lord Your God

Deut. 6:5; Matt. 22:37, 38
Response to the Word

Words and Music by
Jean and Jim Strathdee

Love the Lord your God _____ with

all your heart. _____ Love the Lord your

God _____ with all your soul. _____

Love the Lord your God _____ with all

your mind. _____ Love the Lord your

God _____ with all that you are. _____

96.   LOVE THE LORD YOUR GOD

What Does the Lord Require?

Micah 6:8
Response to the Word/Departing/Ordination

Words and Music by
Jim Strathdee
Adapted by
Linda White

97.   WHAT DOES THE LORD REQUIRE?

The River Is Here

John 4:13–14; 7:37–38; Rev. 22:1–3
Response to the Word

Words and Music by
Andy Park

1. Down the moun-tain the riv - er__ flows
2. The riv - er of God ___ is teem-ing with life
3. Up to the moun-tain we love to__ go

and it brings re - fresh - ing wher - ev - er it goes.
and all who touch it can be __ re - vived; and
to find the pres - ence __ of __ the Lord. A -

Through the val - leys and o - ver the fields the
those who lin - ger on this riv - er's shore will
long the banks of the riv - er we run, we

riv - er is rush-ing and the riv - er is here. The
come back thirst - ing for more of the Lord. The
dance with laugh - ter giv-ing praise to the Son. The

riv - er of God sets our feet a - danc - ing, the

riv - er of God   fills our hears with cheer.   The

riv - er of God   fills our mouths with laugh - ter, and

3rd time continue

we re - joice   for the riv - er is here.

and we re - joice   for the riv - er is here.

Center of My Life

Psalm 16
Prayer

Words and Music by
Paul Inwood

99. CENTER OF MY LIFE

Dona Nobis Pacem

Prayer

Music: Unknown

*Pronounced "pachem." The Latin phrase means "Grant us peace."

In His Presence

Prayer

Words and Music by
Dick and Melodie Tunney

Asus A7	G/D	D	D/F♯	G/A	G

1. In his pres - ence ____ there is com - fort, __
2. In your pres - ence ____ there is com - fort, __

B/F♯ Em   Em/D   C G/B A7 A/G

____ In his pres - ence ____ there is peace. ____
____ In your pres - ence ____ there is peace. ____

D/F♯   G   D/F♯

When we seek the Fa - ther's heart   We will find such bless'd as -
When we seek to know your heart   We will find such bless'd as -

Bm   Em   Asus A7 G/A   D

sur - ance, In the pres - ence of the Lord. ____
sur - ance, In your ho - ly pres - ence, Lord. ____

Gentle Shepherd, Come and Lead Us

John 10:1–30
Prayer

Words and Music by
Gloria and William Gaither

F   G9

Gen - tle Shep - herd, ____ come and lead us, ____

102. GENTLE SHEPHERD, COME AND LEAD US

God, In Your Loving Mercy

Prayer

Words and Music by
Jim Strathdee

God, in your lov - ing mer - cy, hear our prayer.

Healer of My Soul

Isa. 57:18; Matt. 13:1–9, 18–23
Prayer

Words and Music by
John Talbot

1. Heal - er of my soul, _____
2. Keep - er of my soul, _____

Keep me at ev - en', ____ Keep me at
On rough course far - ing. ____ Help __ and

morn - ing, ____ Keep me at noon, Heal - er
safe - guard my means __ this night, Keep - er

103. GOD, IN YOUR LOVING MERCY   104.   HEALER OF MY SOUL

104. HEALER OF MY SOUL

God of Mercy

Prayer

Words and Music by
Bob Hurd

Hear our prayer. Hear our prayer.

Hear our prayer. Hear us, O

God of mer - cy, hear our prayer.

God of mer - cy, hear our prayer.

105. GOD OF MERCY

Hear Us, O God (Oyenos, Mi Dios)

Prayer

Words by Owen Alstott, Spanish trans. by Mary F. Reza
Music by Bob Hurd and Owen Alstott

1. Hear us, O God, Hear us, O God.
2. O - ye - nos, mi Dios, O - ye - nos, mi Dios.

repeat several times

Lis - ten to your peo ple. Hear us, O God.
Lis - ten to your peo - ple. O - ye - nos, mi Dios.

106. HEAR US, O GOD (OYENOS, MI DIOS)

In the Secret

Phil. 3:10–14
Prayer

Words and Music by
Andy Park

107. IN THE SECRET

Spirit, Now Live in Me

Matt. 3:16
Liturgical Year/Pentecost

Words and Music by
Bryan Jeffery Leech, 1976

| C | Am | Fmaj7 | G |

1. O ho-ly Dove of God de-scend-ing,
2. O ho-ly Wind of God now blow-ing,
3. O ho-ly Rain of God now fall-ing,
4. O ho-ly Flame of God now burn-ing,

| C | Am | Fmaj7 | G | C/E |

you are the love that knows no end-ing,
you are the seed that God is sow-ing,
you make the Word of God en-thrall-ing,
you are the power of Christ re-turn-ing,

| F | C/E | Am | Dm | G/B | C |

all of our shat-tered dreams you're mend-ing:
you are the life that starts us grow-ing:
you are that in-ner voice now call-ing:
you are the an-swer to our yearn-ing:

| Dm7 | F/G | G7 | C | Am | Fmaj7 | Gsus | G | C |

Spir-it, now live in me.
Spir-it, now live in me.
Spir-it, now live in me.
Spir-it, now live in me.

108. SPIRIT, NOW LIVE IN ME

Make Me a Channel of Your Peace

John 14:23–28; Rom. 14:13–19
Prayer

Prayer of St. Francis
Music by Sebastian Temple

109. MAKE ME A CHANNEL OF YOUR PEACE

To be un - der - stood as to un - der - stand, ___

___ To be loved as to love with all my soul. ___

3. Make me a chan-nel of your peace. ___ It is in par-don-

ing that we are par - doned, ___ In giv - ing to

all that we re - ceive, ___ And in dy - ing that we're

born to e - ter - nal life. ___

109. MAKE ME A CHANNEL OF YOUR PEACE

Lord, Listen to
Your Children Praying

Ps. 17:6
Prayer

Words and Music by
Ken Medema

Lord, lis-ten to your child-ren pray - ing,

Lord, send your Spir - it in this place;

Lord, lis-ten to your child-ren pray - ing, send us

love, send us pow'r, send us grace. grace,

send us love, send us pow'r, send us grace.

110. LORD, LISTEN TO YOUR CHILDREN PRAYING

O Lord, Hear My Prayer

Ps. 102:1, 2
Prayer

Words and Music by
The Taizé Community

O Lord, hear my prayer, O Lord, hear my prayer.

When I call, an - swer me. O Lord, hear my prayer, O

Lord, hear my prayer. Come and lis - ten to me.

The Lord is my song, the Lord is my praise:

All my hope comes from God. The Lord is my song, the

Lord is my praise: God, the well-spring of life.

111. O LORD, HEAR MY PRAYER

Remember Me

Luke 23:42
Prayer/Holy Week

Words and Music: Traditional

Re - mem - ber me. Re - mem - ber
me. O Lord, re - mem - ber me. _____

The Lord's Prayer

Matt. 6:9–13
Prayer

Music by
Christy Weir

Our Fa - ther, which art in heav - en,

Hal - low - ed be Thy name. Thy king-dom

come. Thy will be done in earth as it

Give Thanks with a Grateful Heart

Ps. 126:3
Offering and Thanksgiving

Words and Music by
Henry Smith

114. GIVE THANKS WITH A GRATEFUL HEART

Everything Is Yours, Lord

1 Chron. 29:9–17; Ps. 138:1–8
Offering and Thanksgiving

Words: Zambian offertory
Arrangement: Geoff Weaver

Ev - 'ry-thing is yours, Lord; ev - 'ry-thing comes from you:
Ta - ta po - ke - le - la If - ya bu - pe fye - su:

all we have we of - fer _____ to you. Ac - cept our love, Lord,
If - yo twa - mi pe - la _____ le - lo. Po - ke - le - le - ni _____

we pray; re - ceive our gifts, Lord, _____ to - day.
ta - ta, Po - ke - le - le - ni _____ le - lo.

Shout for Joy to God

Ps. 100:1–2
Offering and Thanksgiving

Words and Music by
Hal H. Hopson

Shout for joy to God all the earth,

Al - le - lu - ia! Praise the Lord!

115. EVERYTHING IS YOURS, LORD   116.   SHOUT FOR JOY TO GOD

Take Up Your Cross

Matt. 16:24–27; Mark 8:34–38; 10:21; Luke 9:23–25; Eph. 6:11–17
Offering and Thanksgiving

Words and Music by
Kinley Lange

Take up your cross and fol - low me,

lift up the yoke of your sal - va - tion, put on the ar - mor

of the Word, and walk in the Truth and Light.

What would it prof - it you _____ to gain the world

___ for a day? If you would have your life,

___ first, you must give it a - way.

Take up your cross and fol-low me, lift up the yoke of

your sal - va - tion, put on the ar - mor of the Word, and

1. walk in the Truth and Light. *2.* walk in the Truth and

Light, and walk in the Truth and Light.

We Are an Offering

Offering and Thanksgiving

Words and Music by
Dwight Liles

We lift our voi - ces, we lift our hands, we lift our

lives up to you, we are an of - fer - ing. Lord, use our

voi - ces, Lord, use our hands, Lord, use our

lives, they are yours, we are an of - fer - ing.

118.   WE ARE AN OFFERING

118. WE ARE AN OFFERING

Lamb of God
(Good Shepherd Mass)

John 1:29
Communion/Agnus Dei

Music by Owen Alstott
Good Shepherd Mass

Lamb of God, you take a - way the

sins of the world: have mer - cy on us.

Lamb of God, you take a - way the

sins of the world: have mer - cy on us.

Lamb of God, you take a - way the

sins of the world: grant us peace.

119. LAMB OF GOD (GOOD SHEPHERD MASS)

Lamb of God

1 Peter 1:18–19
Communion/Agnus Dei

Words and Music by
Twila Paris

1. Your only Son, no sin to hide, But you have sent him from your side, To walk up-on this guilt-y sod, And to be called the Lamb of God.
2. Your gift of love, they cru-ci-fied, They laughed and scorned him as he died. The hum-ble King they named a fraud And sac-ri-ficed the Lamb of God.
3. I was so lost, I should have died, But you have brought me to your side, To be led by your staff and rod, And to be called a lamb of God.

Refrain

O Lamb of God, sweet Lamb of God, I love the ho-ly Lamb of God! O wash me in his pre-cious blood, My Je-sus Christ the Lamb of God.

120. LAMB OF GOD

Agnus Dei

John 1:29, 36
Communion

Music by
The Iona Community

Among Us and before Us

Matt. 26:26; 1 Cor. 11:23–26
Communion
Response to Pardon/Before Gospel/After Sermon/General Praise

Words and Music by
The Iona Community
Tune: *Gatehouse* (JLB)

	G		Bm		Em		Am	
1. A -	mong	us	and	be -	fore	us,	Lord,	you
2. Who	dare	say	no,	when	such	is	your	re -
3. Who	dare	say	no,	when	such	is	your	in -
4. Who	dare	say	no,	when	such	is	your	re -
5. No	more	we	hes - i -	tate	and	won - der		

D	D7		G		Em7		Am	
stand	With	arms	out - stretched and				bread and	
solve	Our	worst	to	wit - ness,			suf - fer	
tent	To	love	the	selves	we		fam - ish	
quest	That	each	a - round	your			ta - ble	
why;	No	more	we	stand	in -		dif - f'rent,	

/C		Am/D	D		G		Bm	
wine	at	hand.	Con -	front - ing	those	un -		
and	ab -	solve,	Our	best	to	raise	in	
and	re -	sent,	To	cra - dle	our	un -		
should	be	guest,	That	here	the	an - cient		
scared	or	shy.	Your	in - vi -	ta -	tion		

122. AMONG US AND BEFORE US

Em	Am	D	D7		G

wor - thy of a crumb, You ask that
lives by God for - giv'n, Our souls to
cer - tain - ties and fear, To kin - dle
word should live as new: "Take, eat and
leads us to say yes, To meet you

Em7	Am	C/D	G (C2/D)

to your ta - ble we should come.
fill on earth with food from heav'n?
hope as you in faith draw near?
drink— all this is meant for you"?
where you nour - ish, heal and bless.

Bread, Blessed and Broken

1 Cor. 11:24
Communion

Words and Music by
Michael B. Lynch

123. BREAD, BLESSED AND BROKEN

Great Thanksgiving (Land of Rest)

Communion/Great Thanksgiving

Music adapted by
Marcia Pruner, 1980

1. Ho - ly, ho - ly, ho - ly Lord,
2. Bless - ed is he who comes

God of pow-er and might, _____ heav-en and earth are
in the name of the Lord. Ho - san - na in the

full of your glo - ry. Ho - san - na in the high - est.
high - est, _ Ho - san - na in the high - est.

Leader: You are holy, O God of majesty, and blessed is your Son our Lord . . .
Great is the mystery of faith.

Christ has died, Christ is ris - en,

Christ will come a - gain. Christ has died,

Christ is ris - en, Christ will come a - gain.

Leader: Gracious God, pour out your Holy Spirit upon us . . .
Through Christ, with Christ, in Christ, in the unity of the Holy Spirit,
all glory and honor are yours, almighty Father, now and forever.

A - men, A - men, A - men.

124. GREAT THANKSGIVING (LAND OF REST)

Great Thanksgiving

Communion/Great Thanksgiving

Words and Music by
Leon Roberts

Ho - ly, ho - ly, ho - ly Lord,
God of pow'r and might: _____
Heav'n and earth are full of your glo - ry. Ho -
san - na in the high - est. _____
Bless - ed is he who comes in the Lord's name. Ho -
san - na in the high - est.
Bless - ed is he who comes in the Lord's name. Ho -
san - na in the high - est. _____

125. GREAT THANKSGIVING (Roberts)

Leader: You are holy, O God of majesty, and blessed is your Son our Lord . . .
Great is the mystery of faith.

Christ has died, Christ is ris - en,

Christ will come a - gain. _____

Christ has died, Christ is ris - en,

Christ will come a - gain. _____

Leader: Gracious God, pour out your Holy Spirit upon us . . .
Through Christ, with Christ, in Christ, in the unity of the Holy Spirit,
all glory and honor are yours, almighty Father, now and forever.

A - men, A - men,

A - men, A - men, A - men,

A - men, A - men,

A - men, A - men. _____

125. GREAT THANKSGIVING (Roberts)

Come, Share the Lord

Luke 22:17
Communion

Words and Music by
Jeffery Leech

1. We gath-er here in Je-sus' name,
2. He joins us here, he breaks the bread,
3. We'll gath-er soon where an-gels sing;

his love is burn-ing in our hearts like liv-ing flame;
the Lord who pours the cup is ris-en from the dead;
we'll see the glo-ry of our Lord and com-ing King;

for through his lov-ing Son the Fa-ther makes us one:
the one we love the most is now our grac-ious host:
now we an-tic-i-pate the feast for which we wait:

Come, take the bread, come, drink the wine, come, share the Lord.

1. No one is a strang-er here, ev-'ry-one be-longs.
2. We are now a fam-i-ly of which the Lord is head.

Find-ing our for-give-ness here, we in turn for-give all wrongs.
Through un-seen, he meets us here in the break-ing of the bread.

126. COME, SHARE THE LORD

Eat This Bread and Never Hunger

Mark 10:46–52; John 4:5–42; 11:1–45
Communion

Words and Music by
Daniel Charles Damon

Eat this bread and nev - er hun - ger;

Drink this cup and nev - er thirst. Christ in -

vites us to the ta - ble where the last be - come the first.

1. Ask - ing for a cup of wa - ter, Je - sus
2. Walk - ing down a des - ert high - way, Je - sus
3. Weep - ing for his friend at grave - side, Je - sus

touched for - bid - den ground; and the wo - man,
healed a man born blind; soon the man be -
felt the pain of death; yet he knew God's

with a ques - tion, told the world what she had found.
came a wit - ness, to the truth we seek and find.
power to wak - en, liv - ing wa - ter, liv - ing breath.

127. EAT THIS BREAD AND NEVER HUNGER

I Am the Bread of Life

John 6:35, 51, 54
Communion

Words adapt. S. Suzanne Toolan
Music by S. Suzanne Toolan

1. "I am the bread of life. You who
2. "The bread that I will give is my
3. "Un - less _____ you _____ eat of the
4. "I am the res - ur - rec - tion,
5. Yes, Lord, _____ I be - lieve that

come to me shall not hun - ger, and who be -
flesh for the life of the world, _____ and if you
flesh of the Son of Man _____ and _
I _____ am the life. _____ If you be -
you _____ are the Christ, _____ the _

lieve in me shall not thirst. No one can come to
eat _____ of this bread, you shall live for -
drink _____ of his blood, and drink _____ of his
lieve _____ in _____ me, e - ven _ though you
Son _____ of _____ God, who _____ has _

me un - less the Fa - ther beck - ons."
ev - er, you shall live for - ev - er."
blood, you shall not have life with - in you."
die, _____ you shall live for - ev - er."
come in - to _____ the _ world.

128. I AM THE BREAD OF LIFE

"And I will raise you up, and I will raise you up, and I will raise you up on the last day."

In the Singing

Communion

Words by Shirley Erena Murray
Music by Carlton R. Young

1. In the sing-ing, in the si-lence, in the hands ex-pec-tant, o-pen, in the bless-ing, in the break-ing, in the Pres-ence at this ta-ble— Je-sus Christ, Je-sus Christ, be the wine of grace:

2. In the ques-tion, in the an-swer, in the mo-ment of ac-cep-tance, in the heart's cry, in the heal-ing, in the cir-cle of your peo-ple— Je-sus Christ, Je-sus Christ, be the bread of peace.

129. IN THE SINGING

One Bread, One Body

John 17:13–23
Communion

Words and Music by
John Foley, S.J.

130. ONE BREAD, ONE BODY

Partakers of the Holy Food

Communion

Words and Music by
Kevin Boyd

1. Par - tak - ers   of   the   Ho - ly   Food,
2. Re - ceiv - ers   of   the   Bread   and   Wine,

Our spir - its   filled,   our   lives   re - newed.   We will
We are the   branch - es,   Christ   the   vine.

wor - ship   God   as   One.   Might-y   things   our   Lord   has

done!   Christ was   brok - en,   Christ   was   raised!

We   give   our   lives   in   love   and   praise.

131.   PARTAKERS OF THE HOLY FOOD

We Remember You

Luke 22:14–20; 1 Cor. 11:23–26; Rev. 5:12–14
Communion

Words and Music by
Walt Harrah

1. We re - mem - ber you, ___
2. Pre - cious ris - en Lamb, ___

We re - mem-ber you. ___ By your sac - ri -
Je - sus, who was slain, ___ now en-throned in

fice of love all glo - ry now is
glo - ry, for - ev - er you will

due. At this ta - ble here ___
reign. Glad-ly we em - brace ___

mer - cy hov - ers near. ___ Thanks are of - fered
both these signs of grace. ___

132. WE REMEMBER YOU

up. In this bread and cup we re-mem-ber

you. _____ Thanks are of-fered up.

In this bread and cup we re-mem-ber you.

132.   WE REMEMBER YOU

Come, Holy Spirit

Rom. 8:22–27
Liturgical Year/Spirit/Pentecost

Words and Music by
The Iona Community

Come,   Ho - ly   Spir - it,

grac - ious heaven - ly   dove;   come,   fire   of

love.   love,   come, fire   of   love.

133.   COME, HOLY SPIRIT

As You Travel from This Place

Departing/Benediction

Words and Music by
Jim Strathdee

As you trav-el from this place our love is

with you, When you jour-ney near at hand or far a-

broad. All the life we've shared to-geth-er will con-

tin-ue, As you grow in the know-ledge,

learn of the wis-dom, and live in the spir-it of our God.

134. AS YOU TRAVEL FROM THIS PLACE

Dance with the Spirit

Departing

Words and Music by
Jim Strathdee

Dance with the Spir - it ear - ly in the morn - in',

walk with the Spir - it through-out the long day.

Work and hope for the new life a - born - in', lis -

- ten to the Spir - it to show you the way.

Descant

O _____ Spir - it come, come-a to - day,

O _____ Spir - it come, come-a my way.

135. DANCE WITH THE SPIRIT

Freely, Freely

Matt. 10:8b
Departing/Forgiveness/Offering

Music by
Carol Owens

1. God for-gave my sin in Je-sus'
2. All ___ pow'r is giv'n in Je-sus'

name. I've been born a-gain in Je-sus'
name, in ___ earth and heav'n in Je-sus'

name. And in Je-sus' name I come to
name. And in Je-sus' name I come to

you to share his love as he told me to.
you to share his pow'r as he told me to.

He said, "Free-ly, free-ly, you have re-ceived,

free-ly, free-ly give. Go in my name, and be-

cause you be-lieve, oth-ers will know that I live."

136. FREELY, FREELY

No One Will Ever Be the Same

Departing

Words and Music by
The Iona Community
Tune: *Roystonhill* (JLB)

		G	C	Bm7	C
1. We're going to	shine	like	the	sun	in the
2. We're going to	learn	from	the	poor	in the
3. We're going to	walk	with	the	weak	in the
4. We're going to	drink	new __	wine	in the
5. And _____ it	all	starts __	now	in the

King-dom of Heav - en, shine like the sun in the
King-dom of Heav - en, learn from the poor in the
King-dom of Heav - en, walk with the weak in the
King-dom of Heav - en, drink new __ wine in the
King-dom of Heav - en, all starts now in the

King-dom of Heav-en; we're going to shine like the sun in the
King-dom of Heav-en, we're going to learn from the poor in the
King-dom of Heav-en, we're going to walk with the weak in the
King-dom of Heav-en, we're going to drink new __ wine in the
King-dom of Heav-en, and it _____ all starts now in the

King-dom of Heav - en and no one will ev - er be the same.
King-dom of Heav - en and no one will ev - er be the same.
King-dom of Heav - en and no one will ev - er be the same.
King-dom of Heav - en and no one will ev - er be the same.
King-dom of Heav - en and no one will ev - er be the same.

137. NO ONE WILL EVER BE THE SAME

And it's all in Je-sus' name; and it's all in Je-sus' name; yes it's all in Je-sus' name that no one will ev-er be the same.

Go with God

Rom. 8:14
Departing/Benediction

Words and Music by
Isaiah Jones, Jr.

Go with God. Go with God. As you leave this place, go with God. God will di-rect your way, God will light ev-'ry day. As you leave this place, go with God.

138. GO WITH GOD

The Tools of the Trade

Eph. 6:11–20
Departing

Words and Music by
Kinley Lange

1. All a - round us there is beau-ty and
2. As a car - pen - ter con - sid - ers the

kind-ness and love and the joy of God's cre -
dwell-ing to build, stud-ied eye up - on God's

a - tion. There is al - so des - pair and de -
plan, she takes cour-age and pride in the

cep - tion and pain and an ar - my of temp -
tools at her side and the strength in her own

ta - tion. How shall we live as
hands. _____ How will she make a

child-ren of God and ___ walk where Je - sus
build-ing to rise plumb and square in God's kind

139. THE TOOLS OF THE TRADE

139. THE TOOLS OF THE TRADE

God's Love Made Visible

John 1:1–14; 3:16
Liturgical Year/Advent

Words by Iola Brubeck, 1975
Music by Dave Brubeck, 1975

1. God's love made vis-i-ble! In-com-pre-hen-si-ble!
He is in-vin-ci-ble! His love shall reign!
From love so boun-ti-ful, bless-ings un-count-a-ble,
make death sur-mount-a-ble! His love shall reign!
Joy-ful-ly pray for peace and good will.
All of our yearn-ing he will ful-fill.
Live in a lov-ing way. Praise him for ev-'ry day.
O-pen your hearts and pray. His love shall reign!

2. God gave his Son to us to dwell as one of us,
His bless-ing un-to us! His love shall reign!
To Him all hon-or bring, heav-en and earth will sing,
prais-ing our Lord and King! His love shall reign!
O-pen all doors this day of his birth,
all of good will in-her-it the earth.
His star will al-ways be guid-ing hu-man-i-ty
through-out e-ter-ni-ty! His love shall reign!

140. GOD'S LOVE MADE VISIBLE

There Is a Longing

Isa. 11:1–10; Rom. 15:12
Liturgical Year/Advent

Words and Music by
Anne Quigley

Soon and Very Soon

Rev. 22:20
Liturgical Year/Funeral/Advent

Words and Music by
Andraé Crouch

1. Soon and ver - y soon, we are going to see the King.
2. No more cry-ing there, we are going to see the King.
3. No more dy-ing there, we are going to see the King.

Soon and ver - y soon, we are going to see the King.
No more cry - ing there, we are going to see the King.
No more dy - ing there, we are going to see the King.

Soon and ver - y soon, we are going to see the King.
No more cry - ing there, we are going to see the King.
No more dy - ing there, we are going to see the King.

Hal - le - lu - jah! Hal - le - lu - jah! We're
Hal - le - lu - jah! Hal - le - lu - jah! We're
Hal - le - lu - jah! Hal - le - lu - jah! We're

1., 2., 3.

going to see the King!
going to see the King!
going to see the King!

142. SOON AND VERY SOON

4. Soon and ver - y soon, we are going to see the King.

Soon and ver - y soon, we are going to see the King.

Soon and ver - y soon, we are going to see the King.

Hal-le - lu - jah! Hal-le-lu - jah! We're going to see the King.

Hal-le - lu - jah! Hal-le-lu - jah! We're going to see the King.

Hal-le - lu - jah! Hal-le-lu - jah! We're going to see the

King!

142. SOON AND VERY SOON

Emmanuel, Emmanuel

Matt. 1:18–25
Liturgical Year/Advent

Words and Music by
Bob McGee

Em - man - u - el, Em - man - u - el, his name is called Em - man - u - el. God with us, re - vealed in us, his name is called Em - man - u - el.

I Am the Light of the World

John 8:12
Liturgical Year/Christmas/Justice

Words and Music by
Jim Strathdee

"I am the light of the world! You peo - ple come and fol - low me!" If you

144. I AM THE LIGHT OF THE WORLD

Hosanna

Mark 11:1–11
Liturgical Year/Palm Sunday/Christ the King

Words and Music by
Carl Tuttle

1. Ho - san - na! Ho - san - na! Ho -
2. Glo - ry! Glo - ry!

san-na in the high - est! Ho - san - na! Ho -
Glo-ry to the King of kings! Glo - ry!

san - na! Ho - san - na in the high - est!
Glo - ry! Glo - ry to the King of kings!

Lord, we lift up your name, With hearts full of praise;

Be ex - alt - ed, oh Lord, my God! Ho -

san-na in the high - est! Ho -
Glo-ry to the King of Kings! Be ex -

alt-ed, oh Lord, my God! Ho - san-na in the high - est!

Jesus Took a Towel

John 13:3–10
Liturgical Year/Footwashing/Maundy Thursday

Words and Music by
Chrysogonus Waddell, OCSO, 1968

Come and See

Matt. 27:27–44; Mark 15:16–32; Luke 23:8–11, 35–39; John 19:5, 17
Liturgical Year/Good Friday

Words and Music by
Graham Kendrick

1. Come and see, come and see, come and
2. Come and weep, come and mourn for your
3. Man of heav'n, born to earth to re -

see the King of love, see the pur - ple robe and
sin that pierced him there so much deep - er than the
store us to your heav'n, here we bow in awe be -

crown of thorns he wears. _____ Sol - diers mock,
wounds of thorn and nail. _____ All our pride,
neath your search - ing eyes. _____ From your tears

ru - lers sneer, as he lifts the cru - el cross,
all our greed, all our fall - en - ness and shame,
comes our joy. From your death our life shall spring.

lone and friend-less now, he climbs to - wards the hill. _____
and the Lord has laid the pun - ish - ment on him. _____
By your re - sur - rec - tion pow - er we shall rise. _____

147. COME AND SEE

We wor-ship at your feet, where wrath and mer-cy

meet, and a guilt-y world is washed by love's pure

stream. _____ For us he was made sin, oh,

help me take it in. Deep wounds of love cry

out, "Fa-ther for-give." _____ I wor - ship, I

wor - ship the Lamb _____ who was slain.

Glory

Luke 2:13–14; John 1:10, 29, 36
Liturgical Year/Easter

Words and Music by
Danny Daniels

148. GLORY

You Are Mighty

Matt. 28:1–20; Mark 16:1–6; Luke 24:1–9, 34; John 20:1–19
Liturgical Year/Easter

Words and Music by
Craig Musseau

You are might - y, you are ho - ly,

you are awe - some in your pow - er.

You have ris - en, you have con - quered, you have beat -

(repeat first time only)

- en the power of death.

Hal - le - lu - jah, we will re - joice.

Hal - le - lu - jah, we will re -

149. YOU ARE MIGHTY

149. YOU ARE MIGHTY

He Is Lord

Phil. 2:10–11
Liturgical Year/Easter

Author/Composer unknown

1. He is Lord, he is Lord!

He is ris - en from the dead, and he is Lord!

Ev - 'ry knee shall bow, ev - 'ry tongue con - fess

that Je - sus Christ is Lord!

2. He is love, he is love!

He has shown us by his life that he is love!

All his peo - ple sing with one voice of joy

that Je - sus Christ is love!

3. He is life, he is life!

He has died to set us free and he is life!

And he calls us all to live ev - er - more,

for Je - sus Christ is life.

150. HE IS LORD

Come, Spirit, Come

John 16:12–15
Liturgical Year/Pentecost

Words and Music by
Walt Harrah

Come, Ho - ly Spir - it, dwell here a -

mong us. We need your pow - er,

your heal - ing grace. Show us your fa - vor,

grant us your pres - ence as you have

prom - ised. Come, Spir - it, come. come.

Come, rush - ing wind, come ho - ly fire,

151. COME, SPIRIT, COME

here and now de - scend.   O breath of God, O

per - fect peace, re - vive us once a - gain. ___

come.   As you have prom - ised,

come, Spir - it, come.

151. COME, SPIRIT, COME

Topical Index

Index of Authors, Composers, and Arrangers

Index of Titles